Chris Waters

Through a Glass, Lately

mudlark

First published by Mudlark Press 2014
in a limited edition of 200
© Chris Waters 2014

ISBN 978-0-9565162-5-1

Printed in Devon by Imprint Digital
Book design by Sally Chapman-Walker

Published and distributed by
Mudlark Press, Littlehempston, Devon

To Sandra
and the branches and buds
of the family trees

To get back before dark
is the art of going

Wendell Berry, *Travelling at Home.*

Contents

ONE

Through a Glass, Lately

Sometimes, returning late,
you cut through
a familiar street

to find yourself
at the lighted windows
of the house of your life.

Shadows, magnified,
cross behind closed curtains:
flicker and murmur –

everyone is here,
in every room.
Your key is long gone,

but look, the nameplate
and the intermittent bell
still announce you:

a curtain shifts
as a backlit, searching face
peers out into your darkness

My Father's Tools

Which I did not inherit, must be floating
debris in some Universe of Lost Things.

Such weights in a boy's hands – the great grappling
Stillsons, and his ponderous mallets,

cones and balls in turned wood forced down into
lead pipes, making python-like extrusions.

The gleam and sweat of copper! And the arcane
heart of it all, his blow-lamp, brass-crafted,

roaring into cobalt spears of melding
flame, scorching as he tallowed the flux

around the burnished joint, the pad smoking.
Lost things will persist in being lost,

yet as I write to meld and torque these lines,
it's strange, this late, to feel his hands in mine.

Mothers

Day by day now
the mothers are leaving:

paper-light on the draught
of a wing-beat,

casting-off the incalculable
weight of their stories,

they rise and scatter
into the illegible dark:

their pages flutter
beyond our outstretched hands.

Thresholds

My father-in-law,
stiff in the Chapel of Rest.
His florid cheeks.

His brow was ice to my touch.

It's there still in the finger-tips —
that knowledge of the cold
at the core.

         *

My Penguin edition
of 'Hadrian's Wall',
with your faded inscription:

for the day we crossed borders

We over-rode the signs,
strayed till we found ourselves
in places we could no longer name.

         *

'Scrabble' with my mother —
our last together.
Her hands crawl across the board.

There are words I'm trying not to make here.

Each letter defies, and hastens
the end of the game: against
all odds, she plays for points.

A Screening

Nights, these days, I'm back in the old
Picture House – the Gaumont or Trocadero –

front row, upstairs, above the smokers:
the Cartoon and the Serial have finished,

and Pathe News begins, with its stringy cockerel,
martial theme, and pukka voice-over;

I'm looking out now for my grandfather,
in the rapid, jaunty footage of khaki London boys

streaming onto troop-trains in 1915,
crowding the camera for a thumbs-up farewell

to the Last of England, before the Channel
and the final fields of France. And if I were

to catch him, freeze-frame him wild-eyed at Loos,
Ypres, or High Wood, what, looking out, and forward,

would he see? Phosphor and cordite: a shaft
of white light slicing through branching smoke,

distant ranks of bleached, staring faces –
and lifetimes later, upstairs, at the front,

me, as in a silent film, mouthing across
battlefields *I know you will survive.*

A Triptych for Edward Thomas

Breath

When that five-nine shell
which stopped your watch
and stole your breath

screamed over,
hit mud then burst,
releasing your hostage air

and all your words
of Oxfordshire
and Gloucestershire,

did they rise
above the dark
and nameless avenues

you'd charted at the Front,
ride a Channel wind,
and come again home

to those valley lanes
you'd mapped on foot,
those ancient roads

of English names
that led you at last
away to France?

Names

We climb Shoulder of Mutton Hill,
following in the ways you came:

such genius of local speech
in the conferring of a name –

even the beeches you once knew
are live with the language of rain.

Loam

A handful of Hampshire loam
for you signified all England –
set you marching away from home.

Scorched trees, night-shelling, light snow:
Arras, the first of two French fields
your eyes and ears must come to know.

No denying what the heart lacks:
you were far from wooded valleys
and the chalk Downs' primal tracks.

And so to Agny – the tended field
of strangely gentled consonants –
where victors mark what time has killed

with white pages of Portland stone:
their chiselled lines are terse – yours
endure, like the touch of English loam.

Memo to Ed. Thomas from the A303

Edward – just to say that en route
to an Oxford study day (on you)
we pull over for a break at a Little Chef:

Stonehenge looms under an embattled
sky, and we tune in to predictions
of extreme weather,

but inside the Inn of Red Lego
all is well for travellers – we have our
burgers and our cappuccinos

and in the aromatised toilets
English farmyard sounds repeat
and repeat on a tape-loop,

24/7, as we now tend to say.
When that downpour descends,
let's meet in the lee of the old barn

on the chalk rise, or by the fallen elm
at the corner of the half-ploughed field:
we'll catch the news of the day

(or the night) you have just walked,
sound you out on the War, ask directions
before we leave Stonehenge.

Spores: 1918

The spores
        of that rare fungus
sprouting on the old

hospital lawn
        may have legged it
from Picardy to Craiglockhart

in the soil lodged
        in a soldier's boot
before tunnelling

into the under-dark
        then exploding
into mute life

so who knows
        what bomb-bursts
are ticking

on the dumbed tongues
        of those who return
unloved by death?

A Distant View of Craiglockhart

Observatory Hill, Edinburgh, and the city
laid beneath us, whole, a perfect model of itself.

We're nearer the heavens now, could chart
constellations if we waited for dark,

or join the astronomers behind their lens
and fall backwards into the infra-red of deep time;

across the valley, high in its own remove,
like dream-battlements of a castle from Grimm,

the old hospital, silent as the city, the heavens,
or history itself: could any curvature

of any lens take the eye back to the night-rage
in its dark panelled rooms, or the ear to the echo

of words exploding across a flare-lit page?

Soldiers in a Wood, with Snow

The camera's eye
is not innocent:
it has found them,
four of them, here,

in a clearing,
their boot-prints diminishing
in its white depth-of-field;
two-tone branches overhang

their frost-coppered faces.
1915. The Eastern Front.
A pause in the proceedings.
Their eyes glint

with the easy challenge
of those who know
there is nothing
they have not already done.

TWO

Field-Notes

A man crosses a wide field
beneath an open sky

he leaves early with little luggage
putting darkness behind him

there is frost or dew or birdsong

he makes footprints in the new grass
that begin to look like tracks

if he hears a melody
he will stop then follow it

perhaps it is in the back of his head
maybe he hears it on the wind

but he follows it through the wide field

Memory and the Mountains

City-pent this last week,
in teeming, history-raddled streets
and the hubbub of peoples,
in heat that never sleeps,
I'm missing the green silence
of the mountains.
        But packing for the next journey,
I retrieve my walking-shoes,
crumpled and powder-white
from our last climb
through the Bulgarian beechwoods:
I'll brush them, hoard the residue,
call it memory-dust.

Istanbul: Prelude

The long day sighs, surrenders its heat;
    evening trams with plaintive bells
bear their homing multitudes back
    to apartments and supper routines.

The fishermen on Galata Bridge
    ply their jostling lines,
pray for the arrival of silver fish
    from the waters of the Golden Horn.

And at the muezzin's wail
    high on the white minaret,
the sky parts, releasing
    the dark-winged birds of paradise.

Etymologies

If I thumb today's mist from 'Skye',
I'm down to the abrasions
of 'Skuye' – and an old note
carrying on wind over waves:
keels scraping on rocky shores,
unsheathings of iron from hide,
throat-cries of fire and ice.

Skye: Notes

Cloud dragging low
over blue islands

Skylark singing high
over gorse

Keel ploughing sharp
over waves

Wind gusting
over roofless crofts

Clans long silenced
under grass

Bees

Incessant in this cornflower-blue July
the buzz and drone of the honey makers
relieving the foxgloves of their gold:
all that they filch will multiply.

India Haiku

women balancing
water-pots — turquoise, scarlet
shawls sway through fields

> buffalo, roped down
> in a pick-up, nostrils wide
> sniffing city air

two Saddhus walk through
traffic — blanket, can and stick —
their calves shadow-thin

> in the dome above
> the Sultan's ancient tomb, our
> whispers multiply

two goats, champing
at the shadow of a tree
where their master sleeps

> cows roaming highway
> in dust and fumes — do you know
> how holy you are?

dragonflies hover
high — on slopes of cloud-mountain
tea-pickers appear

river rune

who moves and always moves
over his own slow silence

who spells secrets
in broken branches, lost leaves

who is stealth
who gives the slip

to the sentries
the stiff reeds, the bent willows

who sleepwalks through darkness
who receives daylight, starlight

and repays it in pieces

Curlew

The curlew's lone call
is a calligrapher's brush:
a single, liquid
stroke and the sand-flats shimmer
into salty light.

Pears: Doyenne du Comice

Three pears in the long grass:

windfalls, landfalls, gravity
has got the better of them:

three anciennes, ripe dowagers
sitting out at the Grand Ball of Life.

Time has loosened their stays:
they bulge generously with their vintage.

They have tasted summer's amours,
love to savour old scandales,

but now it's the season to nod, wink
and tut-tut at the folies of the slender

young, minuetting before them:
three pears, Doyenne du Comice, in the long grass.

A March Lamb

This hour-old, birth-slippery scrawn
is stretched flat-out on his bedding straw,
still sporting his *maillot jaune*;

his mother marks their victory with her tongue,
soothing and goading, licking him warm,
willing him on from merely *born*:

he'll navigate past her milky form –
try for the light at the door of the barn.

The Naming of Woods in the Weald

Is it because
    we cannot know
whose woods
    these are,
or hear their
    yearly secrecies
hoarded in ring
    and root
and high emerging
    leaf; because
even bird
    and wind
cannot decode
    their branching
confederate
    silences,
that we must
    name and name
them, as if,
    obedient in an
echoing dusk,
    they would answer
to our homing call
    of *Puxty, Shoesmith,*
Stivers, Sluice
    or Nap?

Once Given (Kintyre 2011)

In Gannet-Drop-Sound
by Fish-Leap-Point

where evening swallows
zip and spin

something not-quite-wave-like
ripples beyond the rocks:

a wrong-shaped darkness
moils the quicksilver calm,

tumbles over itself,
sculls in and out of vision,

then with a slick tail-whip
is gone, leaving bubbles

(you imagine), widening rings
and a new marking

onto your map of this place:
Otter-Glimpse-Shore,

where the given, once given,
will become the long-hoped,

the long looked-for.

Down the Allotment

Marvell, I think you'd like it here:
we could sit on the old plank bench

beneath the filmy walnut leaves
and listen to the day exhale;

best come at noon, when all goes still,
and the plots subside to silence.

You'll see – last year's seeds, obedient
to their script (you'll not have heard

of DNA) have done it once
again, and scrawl their signatures

with a Tudor flourish of whorls
and curlicues along the rows.

You know this plenitude in a small,
allotted space, so you will hear

the old pavane of all that grows,
moving through its summer progress.

Green thoughts are rife with us these days:
some will dismay you, some amaze;

we'll nip the tops from tangled peas,
then read the scripts of next year's seeds.

THREE

A Dartmoor Tomb

Dark bride
to blackening earth –
a marriage
of four millennia –

exposed again
to bright air
and probing
forensic eyes:

bone-shadow-wife,
peat-smudge,
all but consumed
in your long sleep;

in time we'll view
your grave-gifts
arrayed under
artful lighting,

ponder the odds
on what survives,
while the wind riffs
through the eye

of an amber bead.

A Bend in Norfolk

My old friend, who died too young,
said he saw it coming, in dream

after stubborn dream: glare of moonlight
on tall reeds, a swerve, a scream,

then the plunge into darkness off the road –
a bend in Norfolk, the nightscape

of his repeated end, a place he'd never
been, but clear as a Google download.

The heart needs its saving metaphors,
but life conspires to out-dream us:

old friend – no capers in a midnight car
for you, just a white road through a glare-

white room, tapering towards its end.

Shelley at Lerici

Cypress and pine brood
in muted shadow

above a dawn-lit sea
lapping as if appeased

at the shore where his pyre
crackles and no bird sings:

all songs must here combust,
but ashes may rise like wings.

From a Dartmoor Book of the Dead

Open a field at any page:
you are reading diagonals, runnels
coursing ever downward,
hill-water obeying only its own narrative,
as yet not signifying weeping or grief.

Reed leaves wind-pressed
on an amber pool –
a scatter of down-strokes;
the river breathless,
a babble of cursives refusing
to arrange themselves.

White striae incising
the cuneiform of granite pink and green :
the calligraphies of chance.

November night on the high moor -
the road a sentence spooling without stops.
You would step out into a forest of print.

The only light for black miles:
the Inn on the high ridge.
Woodsmoke, blaze and ember,
the hoof-beat of the Stranger.

The yew in the churchyard
has split open its bindings, time-chapters
exposed to the eye of the wind:

its claw-roots clutch at memories
quiet under the eye of the moon.

Headstones in granite –
blue-fleck and glitter,
riven with signatures:
time-shifts and depositions,
a mason's mark, the algebra of a fading name,
a date that isn't.

Rain side-shifting in columns –
ghost Legion in grey retreat
over the hills.

And the Roll of Honour
in every parish church?
Stories sleeping, waiting for their author:
how to begin to even read such losses?

Red coats hound a red brush
to the very edge of Twisted Wood:
one leap and its flame vanishes
into a tangle of dark – a death deferred.
The Wood is a closed book:
the hounds on the hill are inconsolable.

A sky of blue clearances,
the moor-line one clean uplift:
here is our tabula rasa :
a buzzard soars; today
the dead are not yet invented.

Heptonstall
S.P-H.

Storm clouds scud low, harebells
shimmy in the long grass;
blackened headstones huddle.

You lie, long chambered
in your after-life, earthed
beyond all fire, all grief.

What poet ever courted silence?
The downpour through the yews
roars and roars its syllables.

FOUR

Upshore

If you do return, come again
at low water, when rain clouds brood

over light-filled pools – anywhere
between Crow Point and Pebble Ridge,

or in sight of the old boatyard
with its stoic, bleached timbers;

you'll find these words washed
upshore, among the wrack

and clitter, where samphire has rooted
among brick and slate shards;

some will have lodged in shingle,
wedged where mussels and cockles

lie like opened books; or by the long-
rusted maps of iron, printed

on the wind-ribbed sand.
If you are in ear-shot of the curlew's

thin, single call, you'll know
that they are somewhere near

and you are almost there

Singing Out the Light

Outside the kitchen cocoon
of warmth and simmering aromas

the day subsides to indigo;
winter branches, fine-etched,

loom in the blue; the heart beats slow
and the air is still with absences.

Poised somewhere near, out of sight,
a blackbird, with utter unhurried

clarity, is singing out the light.

An Upturned Boat

For today, let it be enough
that this boat, belly-up
for winter, sea-crazed

and abraded, is angled
into its own pool of shadow
on the shingle bank,

and reveals its perfect lines,
a curvature of lapped planks
culminating in the downstroke

of a keel, which has out-ridden
all caprice of wind and wave:
beside this blue-washed sky,

what other element would it need
now that it is going nowhere
so slowly?

Woman on a Delft Train with White I-Phone

Johannes, you would get her right:
eyes concealed behind designer shades,

the light glancing off the window
as the train purrs toward Amsterdam,

brightening her immaculate phone
where someone from her expensive destination

is texting her, making her suppress a smile,
making her thumb dance on the keypad.

Those tooled leather boots.
That filigree ankle chain.

Night-Watch
After Rembrandt

Curfew – and the Night-Watch, sober elders all,
with their halberds and flickering lamps,

patrol the courtyards and fetid alleyways
of the sleeping city, on the look-out

for all manner of malfeasance in the dark:
so when I dreamed, love, that you had left me,

where were they when needed, why did they not
scotch your vanishing act, how did they not stumble

into the void you left behind?

Chairmaking in Yew
For Nick Kary

But who dreams the bird
in the wild wood

with the berry in its beak
that becomes the tree

that the woodcutter fells
his eyes lit with the form

his hands seek in the wild grain
which he hews and shapes

into this chair, poised now
in the winter gleam

of a quiet room?

Dutch Honey
For Seamus Heaney

You'd be sure to feel at home here
in this low-lying Zeeland farm,

open to an impasto sky
of pigeon-blues: its fields are trim

and the orchards shapely from years
of skillful graft: only the arching,

loaded, walnut tree could tip
the equilibrium.

The bee-master, eighty if a day,
is frail, frugal in speech,

reluctant to say over-much in answer
to our translated questions;

his eyes track the tipsy traffic
of the bees, clamorous at the skeps.

He has out-wintered them from near collapse,
nurtured them through dark, cold days,

so that now, in the cool penumbra
of the barn, the honey jars are set —

composed, clarified, gleaming.

Liminal

As if, skirting the wood
at the margin of the day,
crossing between here and there,

we pause on the chalk track
while light fades to a hush,
and in that space

the nightjars appear,
shadow-flickers spooling
and swooping in the valley

below, an under-glint
as they turn and rise, till one,
black against the sky's last indigo,

wings outstretched, hovers
above our tipped faces,
as if, before night falls,

we too have somehow been seen.

Thanks and Acknowledgements

I would like to acknowledge the editors of the following journals, where some of these poems have previously appeared: *International Psychoanalysis; Acumen Literary Journal; The Edward Thomas Fellowship Newsletter.*

'My Father's Tools' was a finalist prizewinner in the Wivenhoe Poetry competition 2010; 'Our Mothers' was also a finalist prize poem for the Plough Prize 2010.

Warm thanks to friends who have helped by reading some or all of the collection at an earlier stage: Naomi Fabian-Miller, Sandra Greaves, Bridget Thomasin, Bill Eaton and Chris Fogg.

Special thanks to Sandra Law – *la mia prima lettore* – and to Sally Chapman-Walker, designer for Mudlark Press, for her creative eye as a 'book-maker'.

The cover image is a monoprint by Chris Waters – with thanks to the Dartington Printmakers' Workshop.